THE PRACTICE AND POWER OF PRAYER

The
PRACTICE
and
POWER
of
PRAYER

JOHN SUTHERLAND BONNELL

Philadelphia
THE WESTMINSTER PRESS

Library of Congress Catalog Card No.: 54-5654

PRINTED IN THE UNITED STATES OF AMERICA

To
the devoted members of
The Ten Prayer Groups
meeting weekly in
The Fifth Avenue Presbyterian Church
for intercession,
this manual on prayer
is affectionately inscribed

CONTENTS

Introduction   9

1. Prayer — A Limitless Power   21
2. The Science of True Prayer   31
3. Does Anything Happen When You Pray?   41
4. Will Your Prayers for Others Affect Their Lives?   51
5. The Lord's Prayer Interpreted   61
6. Jesus' Prayer in Gethsemane   73
7. Answering Your Questions on Prayer   85

INTRODUCTION

INTRODUCTION

I BELIEVE IN PRAYER. I believe that prayer can become the most important fact in the life of modern-day persons who are willing to put this religious discipline to the test.

The trouble with most people is that they approach the subject of prayer from an academic standpoint. They argue whether or not it is reasonable, whether they can look for results in a world such as ours. They discuss learnedly the pros and cons and do everything except pray.

John R. Mott, on one occasion, said that in his early college days he had grave doubts as to the effectiveness of prayer. He found it difficult to believe that prayer could change either things or persons. He had been imbued with what is sometimes called the "scientific temper," which emphasizes the inexorableness of natural law. To remove the doubts which oppressed his mind, Mott decided to read some books on prayer. He read forty-three. While he found these helpful and sometimes inspiring, they did not resolve his doubts. These were settled only as he abandoned wearisome discussions on prayer and actually began to pray. Far more convincing than a score of arguments in favor of prayer is one meaningful experience of what prayer can actually accomplish.

Many a person has caught a new vision of the possibility of prayer through hearing Dr. E. Stanley Jones tell of what it did for his life. He credits prayer for his complete recovery from a succession of nervous collapses. He had tried both the mountains and the plains of India. He tried furloughs to the United States and other lands. He invoked the skill of medical missionaries and doctors in his homeland — but all to no avail. Finally in desperation, while kneeling in prayer, he offered his life in complete surrender to God. He writes: " A great peace settled into my heart and pervaded me. I knew it was done. Life, abundant life, had taken possession of me." In more than three decades Dr. Jones has not had a single recurrence of the malady which had threatened to end his missionary career.

If in these pages the importance of a practical and experimental approach to prayer is stressed, it is not because we lack an answer to the doubts and questions engendered by the modern scientific spirit. Rather, it is because of the conviction that it is not in this area that most people's difficulties lie.

Some twenty-five years ago Dr. Kirsopp Lake, Professor of Church History at Yale University, wrote, " I do not believe that the religion of tomorrow will have any more place for petition than it will have for any other form of magic." His " religion of tomorrow " is our religion of today, yet millions of people still believe in and practice petitionary prayer. Professor Lake thought that meteorology would kill prayer. If we teach people that a falling barometer portends foul weather and a rising barometer promises that the weather will be fair, how, Dr. Lake asked, can we expect them to retain their faith in prayer? If they accepted the idea that the weather is determined by natural law, would they not assume its operation in all other realms of nature? Apparently Christian scholars have been more concerned than the scientists about natural law.

Just about the time that Kirsopp Lake's views appeared in print another article was published on the subject of prayer. It was written by one of the best known physicists of Britain and dealt with prayer and natural law. It was published in the *Hibbert Journal*. This scientist wrote: " As to what is scientifically possible or impossible, anything not self-contradictory or inconsistent with other truth is possible. Religious people seem to be losing some of their faith in prayer. They think it scientific not to pray in the sense of simple petition, but, so far as ordinary science has anything to say to the contrary, a more childlike attitude might turn out to be truer, more in accordance with the total scheme of things." So Sir Oliver Lodge, the scientist, taught the Christian professor a lesson in faith.

There are probably fewer persons today than at any time in the last hundred years who are ready to believe that God is a prisoner of his own creation, or that nature can resist or nullify his divine will. No longer do we think of God as One who breaks into the universe in order to work his wonders, but rather we think of the universe itself as an expression of the mind and will of God. William Cowper, the English poet, writes:

> " There lives and works
> A soul in all things, and that soul is God.
> The Lord of all Himself, through all diffused,

> Sustains and is the Life of all that lives.
> Nature is but the name for an effect
> Whose cause is God."

No better testing ground for prayer can be found than in one's own personal life. The evidential value of this kind of praying may not always be convincing to others, but to ourselves it comes with overwhelming force. A personal experience will make clear what I mean.

Like many another person who has come to New York from a smaller community, I found myself overpowered by the crowded subways and buses of this teeming city. I disliked being pushed around by people and was annoyed to find myself tightly jammed into a bus or a subway train. The hardest ordeal was always the trip to the Presbyterian Medical Center at 168th Street. The subway was by far the swiftest method of transportation, but it involved a journey of a hundred blocks or more underground. Usually I had to make the trip in the late afternoon and shared the subway with swarms of jostling, perspiring, weary people at the end of a long and exhausting day. The screaming of the wheels on the rails when we struck a curve and the general noise and confusion grated on my soul like sandpaper. Then one day I happened to notice that my hand, holding the strap in the center of a swaying multitude, was lifted up in the attitude of prayer. The thought came to me: " After all, these men and women are God's children and life is pressing hard on many of them. How can I better employ my time than in praying for them and for myself? " From that moment all dread of the subway journey disappeared. I now pray for

those around me and then pray that I myself may receive
the peace of God and carry it to the sick people whom I
shall shortly visit in the hospital. On many occasions I
have come up out of the subway with a mind and heart at
peace and a deep inner stillness such as one might find
through prayer in some cloistered oratory.

It is unfortunate that we have come to think of prayer
as something that is appropriate only to privacy or to the
holy quiet of a church or chapel. There is no predeter-
mined place for prayer and no fixed time. We can pray at
any time in any place. Of course, posture in prayer is not
without importance and the Scriptures stress the prayer
offered reverently on our knees. Jesus knelt in prayer and
sometimes prostrated himself before God. He also prayed
while standing on his feet. Daniel knelt upon his knees
three times a day, with the window in his chamber open
toward Jerusalem. Paul knelt in prayer. In one of his letters the apostle says, " For this cause I bow my knees
unto the Father." Stephen knelt in the hour of his martyr-
dom. Peter knelt in the death chamber where Dorcas lay
in Joppa. When Paul was leaving his friends on the shore
not far from Tyre, the whole congregation knelt as Paul
pronounced a blessing upon them. But this is not the only
attitude we may assume in prayer. We are free to pray in
any posture — seated in a chair, lying on a bed, walking on
the streets of a crowded city, riding in a bus, a taxi, or a
subway.

At this point we do well to hear the testimony of two
masters of the art of prayer. Horace Bushnell said: " I fell
into the habit of talking with God on every occasion. I talk

myself asleep at night and open the morning talking with him." And Sir Thomas Browne, the famous physician of seventeenth century England wrote, " I have resolved to pray more and to pray always, to pray in all places where quietness inviteth, in the house, on the highway, and on the street; and to know no street or passage in this city that may not witness that I have not forgotten God."

It is important, however, that there should also be fixed times and seasons for private devotions. Dr. John Henry Newman well said, " Those who do not pray at stated times in a direct and earnest manner are not likely to pray at other times." We need periodically the spiritual discipline of a reverent posture in prayer.

The most appropriate time for private devotions is generally found to be the morning hour when the mind is alert, the body rested, and the whole day lying before us. Much of the strain and tension will be taken from the day when we begin it with God. Our interpersonal relations will be better. We shall be more patient with people and less vulnerable to affronts from the thoughtless and the unkind.

One of the chief obstacles to our receiving the fullest benefit from prayer is our frequent failure to receive the answer. This is especially true of prayer for the healing peace of God. There are three stages to prayer: first the petition, second the divine response, and third receiving the answer. As Jesus has said: " Every one that asketh receiveth." That is the completed prayer. We too often follow the example of the apostles who prayed for the release of Peter from prison and then left the answer to their prayer knocking at the door vainly seeking admission.

On one occasion a terribly distraught young woman, seventeen years of age, awaited me in the consulting room of our church. She was accompanied by her brother. As soon as he stepped out of the room so that I might talk with her alone, she rose to her feet and began nervously pacing back and forth wringing her hands and saying: " O God, help me! O God, help me! " It was impossible to get her attention, much less to carry on a conversation with her or have her tell me her troubles. As she paced back and forth muttering, sometimes incoherently, her piti-ful pleas, I began to recite in low, even tones God's prom-ises of the gift of his peace: " Peace I leave with you, my peace I give unto you: not as the world giveth, give I unto you. Let not your heart be troubled, neither let it be afraid." " Thou wilt keep him in perfect peace, whose mind is stayed on thee: because he trusteth in thee." " The peace of God, which passeth all understanding." As I continued repeating these words, the girl's agitation gradually subsided, and after a little time she sat down and composed herself to discuss her problems. There is a mys-tical quality, a peace-giving power, in these words of Holy Scripture.

Oftentimes the counselor will himself need the restora-tive power of God's peace. On late afternoons, especially when several interviews have been held in succession, I find myself physically and mentally tired. When still an-other consultant is ushered in, I know it will be necessary for me to replenish depleted resources, so, at some appro-priate point in the interview, I say to this person: " Let

us together draw upon the peace of God. Trust yourself
to the chair in which you are sitting and close your eyes
to shut out the distractions around you." Then I offer this
prayer, saying it very slowly and having the consultant repeat it quietly after me: " O God, who art the source of
all peace, I thank thee for this spiritual gift which thou
hast offered and which I now receive and accept. The
peace of God is flooding my life. The peace of God is
mine. The peace of God is within me. Thou wilt keep me
in perfect peace for my mind is stayed on thee. The peace
of God is now filling me with quietness, relaxation, healing, and spiritual power. I relinquish every anxiety and
care and trust wholly in thee, O God; through Him, who
is the Lord of peace, even Jesus Christ. Amen." This prayer
may be used by anyone and if used with faith in its efficacy,
will bring mental, physical, and spiritual restoration. It
is particularly helpful when one through prayer and confession has exteriorized his repressed emotions and inner
conflicts. It would appear that this experience was not un-
known to Augustine, for he prayed, " Let my heart, this
sea of restless waves, find peace in thee, O God."

Most people when learning how to pray find themselves
completely lacking in the power of concentration. The
mind is always drifting away from the thought of God to
mundane considerations, so they become discouraged and
give up the attempt. But the art of concentration is never
developed quickly. Such an achievement calls for the exercise of patience and perseverance. God, who made the
mind of man, knows full well how difficult it is for his
children to train their minds to disciplined attention.

Wherefore don't let impatience or discouragement rob you of the blessing which prayer brings to those who employ it believingly.

Brother Lawrence, one of the best known men of prayer in Christian history, was for a long time distressed by his inability to concentrate in prayer. To those similarly troubled he said in effect: "Don't be agitated and distressed by such a failure. Call your mind back repeatedly to the contemplation of spiritual things and especially to a realization of God's presence. Don't upbraid or censure yourself. Faithful perseverance will bring rewarding results in the end."

Now as we turn to the greastest master of prayer that the world has ever known and study the model prayer he gave to his disciples, may it be with the petition in our hearts that his followers asked of him: "Lord, teach us to pray."

【1】

PRAYER — A LIMITLESS POWER

" *And I say unto you, Ask, and it shall be given you; seek, and ye shall find; knock, and it shall be opened unto you.*"

LUKE 11:9

【1】

PRAYER – A LIMITLESS POWER

IN THE YEAR 1872, Professor John Tyndall, British philosopher and scientist, came to the United States on a lecture tour. His visit coincided with a period of religious controversy. He entered the conflict, taking the side of scientific skepticism. He declared that prayer is unscientific and purposeless. In defense of his viewpoint, he challenged Christian people to a test. He said: " Go into a hospital ward and divide the patients into two equal groups. Make sure that they have similar illnesses and that they receive the same medical attention, but let Christian people pray for one group and neglect the other. Then we shall see if any improvement is shown in the patients who have been prayed for."

Of course, the test was wholly impractical and one marvels at a man with scientific training suggesting such an absurd project. In the first place, it would be quite impossible to divide a hospital ward into two groups suffering from illnesses of identical severity. In the second place, one couldn't be sure that both groups would have exactly similar medical care. Finally, one could never be certain that the second group was not prayed for by someone, or that the patients did not slip in a few prayers of their own.

If, however, a feasible plan could be devised, religion would not shrink from such an encounter. It is demonstrably true that the prayer of faith possesses powerful therapeutic, that is, healing value.

In view of Professor Tyndall's statement, it may be worth our while to listen to some testimonies to the healing power of prayer — testimonies offered by some of the ablest leaders of medical science in recent centuries.

In the seventeenth century Sir Thomas Browne, one of Britain's most distinguished physicians and a man of letters, wrote a book entitled *Religio Medici* — " The Religion of a Doctor." He writes: " I cannot go to cure the body of my patient but I forget my profession and call upon God for his soul."

As early as the seventeenth century medical science was already becoming aware of the importance to physical well-being of a vital and vigorous spiritual life.

Another witness is Lord Horder, for years physician-in-ordinary to British kings. He writes: " There is a very definite point of contact between religion and medicine. Not only is there no opposition between them, but they can and should be made complementary to each other in relation to the bodily and spiritual portions of a man's life." [1]

He adds that a good doctor will provide a sympathetic atmosphere for the exercise of the patient's faith.

Let us now hear from a psychiatric specialist. I quote the words of Dr. Hyslop, of London's Bethlem Mental

[1] *Psychology for Pastor and People,* by Dr. John S. Bonnell, p. 160. Harper & Brothers, 1948.

Hospital: " As one whose whole life is concerned with the suffering of the human mind, I believe that of all the hygienic measures to counteract depression of spirits and all the miserable results of a distracted mind, I would undoubtedly give first place to the simple habit of prayer." [2]

A final spokesman chosen from the galaxy of available witnesses is Dr. Alexis Carrel, who so often wrote on the subject of prayer and healing. It is not common knowledge that after his death an unpublished manuscript on the subject of prayer was found among his papers. Through the co-operation of his wife it was put into the hands of an English churchman in Surrey, who had it published. I quote from this document: " A doctor who sees a patient give himself to prayer can indeed rejoice. The calm engendered by prayer is a powerful aid to healing." He adds: " It is by prayer that man reaches God and that God enters into him. Prayer appears indispensable to our highest development." [3]

Despite the scorn of Professor Tyndall, the reality and practicability of prayer is abundantly demonstrated and it produces beneficial results in man's physical as well as his spiritual life.

So the truth of Jesus' words has been confirmed in human experience. " Ask, and it shall be given you; seek, and ye shall find; knock, and it shall be opened unto you."

Now let me ask a question: Do Christians, in general,

[2] *Psychology in Service of the Soul,* by Leslie D. Weatherhead, pp. 156, 157. The Macmillan Company, 1930.
[3] *Prayer,* by Dr. Alexis Carrel, pp. 37, 38. Morehouse-Gorham Company, Inc., 1948.

believe this? If by " believe " we mean " the acceptance of a proposition or statement on grounds of authority or evidence," then a large proportion of people do believe. But if, instead of that definition from the Oxford dictionary, we put a deeper content into that word " believe," the result will be quite different. Prayer life, to be effective, needs something more than merely an intellectual acceptance of certain ideas. It requires a conviction so powerful that it moves the will and causes the individual to act upon his conclusions. Only then will prayer produce definite and specific results.

Of the 48,000,000 Protestants in America, what percentage, do you suppose, firmly believe in prayer and daily practice it? I don't know what your guess would be, but on the basis of many years' counseling with thousands of individuals, I should say that the percentage would not exceed twenty-five. Of 48,000,000 Protestants associated with our churches, not more than one in four, in that case, possesses a meaningful prayer life. Prayer is an exercise of the Christian life universally praised but seldom practiced. It is widely commended but shamefully neglected.

Of course, a much larger number of persons " say their prayers," but that's a vastly different matter. It may be nothing more than a carry-over of a childhood habit. That kind of praying lacks vitality, awareness, and reality. People who merely " say their prayers " expect little from them and they receive less. Only the husk of prayer is left. The kernel has long since withered away.

One of the major tragedies of modern Christianity is

this defect. In the absence of vital prayer we are all spiritually poorer. Our churches are depleted in power and the nation lacks the confidence and courage and high morale so sorely needed as we seek to give moral and spiritual leadership to the free peoples of the world.

Our own history affords us a thrilling illustration of what one man can do to rally and inspire and kindle the loyalty of a whole people. Recently I have been reading the comprehensive five-volume biography of George Washington, by Douglas Southall Freeman. There have been times when I have read this biography with misty eyes and with a lump in my throat, asking myself, " How could any one man have accomplished so much? "

Think of that winter of 1777–1778, when the Army was quartered at Valley Forge. Washington's men had been twice defeated. They were ill-fed, ill-housed, with thousands barefooted and in rags. There had been so many desertions that if the Army had kept the field it would have melted away. Washington faced not only the complaints of his men throughout that winter of semistarvation, but the disaffection and sometimes the outright disloyalty of his generals. He met the harsh criticism of the public, who wanted an easy victory, and overmuch meddling from a Congress that had fled in panic from Philadelphia, going into hiding in the vastnesses of central Pennsylvania. One man and one alone held the Government, the Army, and the people steadfastly to their task. That man was George Washington.

Little wonder that the eloquent statesman William

Ewart Gladstone, of Britain, said, " George Washington is the noblest figure that ever stood in the forefront of a nation's life."

Where did Washington obtain this steadfastness of purpose and this courage of soul? Repeatedly he declared that it was Almighty God who sustained and studied him in many a trying hour. By faith and prayer he drew upon inexhaustible moral and spiritual resources. He said that the hand of God was so conspicuous in all his affairs that he would be worse than an infidel if he lacked this faith.

Dr. Freeman tells in memorable words of that dramatic moment when Washington, having won a complete and overwhelming victory and a just and righteous peace, turned back his commission as Commander in Chief of the American Forces to the Congress assembled to receive it. In the closing words of his address he said: " I consider it an indispensable duty to close this last solemn act of my official life by commending the interests of our dearest country to the protection of Almighty God — and those who have the superintendence of them to his holy keeping."

At this point in his address, says Freeman, Washington's voice choked with emotion, and many a spectator of that moving scene, because of his tears, could not even glimpse his hero.

We are living at a time when all that our forefathers gained for us and all that we hold dear is threatened as it has never been since the birth of this nation. We need today in our leaders and among ourselves those qualities of steadfastness, integrity, and courage so conspicuously present in the " Father of Our Country."

Thank God that many of these noble characteristics have already been manifested by our new leader, President Eisenhower. Like Washington, he believes firmly in prayer and in the guidance of Almighty God.

This is amply attested by the moving petition that he composed and read at his inauguration. It is further revealed by his uniting with the National Presbyterian Church at Washington by profession of faith in Christ and by the fact, reported in the press, that the weekly meetings of the President's cabinet are opened by silent prayer.

Not everyone knows that President Eisenhower has long believed in the efficacy of prayer. I cite a notable instance of this from his war experience.

On the night of July 10–11, 1943, a vast armada of 3,000 ships containing 80,000 Allied soldiers sailed across the waters from Malta to the shores of Sicily in a great amphibious operation. General Eisenhower, surrounded by his staff officers, stood on a high hill overlooking Malta harbor. In the light of a full moon shining down on the sea he watched the troop-laden ships weigh anchor and sail out into the mists while squadrons of planes roared into the sky. Deeply moved, Eisenhower sprang to attention and saluted his heroic men. Then he bowed his head in silent prayer — his staff joining him in this brief act of devotion. Turning to an officer beside him, Eisenhower said: " There comes a time when you've used your brains, your training, your technical skill, and the die is cast and the events are in the hands of God, and there you have to leave them."

Well may we thank God for a national leader with a faith like that. I predict that we are going to witness a nation-wide revival of prayer. Already prayer groups are being formed in hundreds of churches and some have been organized in business offices. Let the whole Church of Jesus Christ marshal its forces for a great crusade of prayer. Let us put God to the test and he will not fail us. Then and then only will our churches become pulsating centers of spiritual power throughout the nation. Then shall we be garrisoned to meet whatever dangers and difficulties lie ahead, for, as was said by an apostle of Christ centuries ago, " If God be for us, who can be against us? "

❨2❩

THE SCIENCE OF TRUE PRAYER

" If a son shall ask bread of any of you that is a father, will he give him a stone?"

LUKE 11:11

{2}

THE SCIENCE OF TRUE PRAYER

Dr. Leslie D. Weatherhead, minister of the City Temple, London, recalls that as a boy of fifteen he experienced a grave disappointment in prayer. He very much wanted to pass a matriculation examination. Having read in the Bible that whatever we ask in Jesus' name we shall receive, and thinking that this means anything we may desire, he prayed fervently for success in his examination. When the results were announced, he found that he had failed. His faith in prayer was sadly shattered.

Do you recall the case of little Kathy Fiscus, of California, who, while playing in a field, fell into a narrow open well? Frantically, relays of workers dug into the earth to release her. The story was front-page news. Millions of people prayed for her safety. When at last the rescuers reached her, she was dead. Indeed she had been already dead for some hours while prayers were being offered for her safety. All across the nation multitudes of people wondered about prayer because of their disappointment that these petitions were not answered.

Now does this mean that it is vain to expect an answer to prayer — that God will not or cannot hear our suppli-

cations? Or does it mean that we have confused and per-
verted notions of what prayer really is? Does the trouble
lie with prayer itself, or is it due, rather, to our methods of
praying and the kind of things for which we pray?

Prayer is the greatest single reservoir of spiritual power
available to man — yet it remains largely untapped. Perhaps the best method of dealing with this complex issue
is to clear away the tangle of misunderstanding that clut-
ters our pathway. Let us begin by noting some of the
things that true prayer is not.

First, it is not a blank check on which God's signature
appears, guaranteeing us anything on which we may set
our hearts. Infinite wisdom does not put itself at the mercy
of the whims and foibles of finite men and women.

Second, prayer is not a rabbit's foot or other charm, war-
ranted to preserve us from misfortune. During the last war
some such talisman was carried by many soldiers to bring
them good luck. This was not an expression of faith. It
was a reversion to primitive superstition.

Third, it is not a " parachute project," to be reserved for
use in some extreme emergency. Dame Quickly, in Shake-
speare's play, says of the dying Falstaff: " Now I, to comfort him, bid him a' should not think of God; I hoped
there was no need to trouble himself with any such
thoughts *yet*."

Fourth, prayer is not a child's letter to Santa Claus. It
is not just an appeal devoted to securing " things." This
type of prayer is often given a central place in our thinking. While the saints and seers and mystics, who are ex-
perts in prayer, regard petition for material things as legiti-

mate, they unfailingly relegate it to a secondary place.

Fifth, true prayer is never an attempt to change God's mind, or to bring him around to our way of thinking. It is not directed to overcoming the divine reluctance. It is not a campaign to persuade God to do something he otherwise would have left undone.

These five fallacious ways of looking at prayer are by no means exhaustive, but their removal will help to clear the way for a constructive, true, and Christian understanding of what prayer really is.

That is enough of negatives. Let us now look at the positive side of the problem. Is there a science of true prayer? We are using the word here in the sense in which Webster's dictionary defines science: " Accumulated and accepted knowledge which has been systematized and formulated with reference to the discovery of general truths."

Let me make a positive affirmation which I believe to be unfailingly true of prayer: *No true prayer ever goes unanswered*. But isn't this a contradiction of human experience? Don't we sing in one of our hymns, " Teach me the patience of unanswered prayer "?

It is quite true that a particular request that has been made in prayer may be denied, but true prayer itself never goes unheeded. Unfailingly it brings a response from God. That divine response belongs to the very essence of prayer.

What are the general truths at which we arrive after formulating our knowledge of prayer?

First, no true prayer can ever go unanswered, because it is not a true prayer unless in it we confront God and have fellowship with him. There is no gift of which the

human imagination can conceive or that we can ask of
God greater than this, that in prayer we meet him and
have converse with him.

If Christian people could but realize this, if they could
grasp this truth, it would revolutionize their thinking on
prayer. No longer would it seem a drab, dull, pedestrian
experience. It would begin to glow with unwonted radi-
ance. Then how insignificant would seem those petty little concerns that we so often bring to him in the light of
one tremendous, overpowering fact — that in prayer we
meet God face to face.

Do you recall an incident from the life of Phillips
Brooks, of Boston? A Harvard student sought an interview with him to get help with a personal problem. He
spent an hour in the study of the great preacher. When he
returned to his dormitory, a fellow student asked, " Oh,
what did Dr. Brooks say about your problem? "

" Do you know," said the student, " I forgot to mention
it? It didn't seem to matter anyway when I talked with
Phillips Brooks."

You see, the contagious power of a radiant and victorious personality lifted that boy far above his problem so
that it didn't matter any longer. And what may not happen to you and me when we come into the presence of the
eternal God? That encounter with a holy God can cleanse
and strengthen, can exalt and redeem us, so that the problem no longer matters.

Augustine was at the heart of the issue when he prayed,
" Give me thine own self, without which, though thou
shouldest give me all that ever thou hadst made, yet could

not my desire be satisfied."

Thomas a Kempis wrote, " It is too small and unsatis-factory, whatsoever thou bestowest on me, apart from thy-self."

And George Matheson, the blind preacher of Scotland who wrote " O Love That Wilt Not Let Me Go," cried out, " It is thee and not thy gifts I crave."

This has ever been the experience of the greatest saints. The biographer of Saint Francis of Assisi writes that this noble and selfless man prayed all night on one occasion uttering but one word at intervals: " God . . . God . . . God." How irrelevant would a minor personal problem or a temporal need appear in the light of an experience so transcendent and so purifying as this!

This is exactly what we need today — something that will save us from the meaninglessness of existence, that will lift us above the trivia of life — that in a world of ceaseless tensions and change and decay we shall realize that " there are values in life that don't fluctuate with the Dow-Jones averages." So shall we know that high above the strutting tyrants of our time is a sovereign God, and that those who live in fellowship with him are undefeat-able.

The Christian revelation declares that, living on this little island in the sky that we call our world, we are not confronted by a universe unfriendly, meaningless, impla-cable, that will finally grind us back into dusty death, but that at the very heart of creation is One who upholds all things by the word of his power and who is patient, loving, just, holy, who knows his human children one by one and loves them with an everlasting love.

On one occasion when our Lord was discussing prayer with his disciples, he suggested that if they wished to understand God's relation to man they should think of a kindly and just human father. "If a son shall ask bread of any of you that is a father, will he give him a stone? or if he ask a fish, will he for a fish give him a serpent? or if he shall ask an egg, will he offer him a scorpion?"

In each case the thing asked for looks like the substitute mentioned by Jesus. A stone would closely resemble a loaf of Palestine bread. The serpent could readily look like a fish, and a scorpion like an egg. "Would a father deceive his child," Jesus asks, "and give him something that would destroy him? Well then, if a human father with all his weaknesses and sins, plans the best for his children; how much more," said Jesus, "shall your Heavenly Father give the Holy Spirit with his guidance and counsel to them that ask him?"

But what if the son had asked his father for a stone in place of bread? Would he have given it to him? One fault of modern praying is that we are continually asking God for stones instead of bread, and we think our prayers are unanswered because he insists on giving us bread rather than a stone.

Here, then, we are at the heart of prayer. The God whom you meet is your Heavenly Father. Wherefore, as his child, bring all your problems, all your desires, all your longings to him, asking him to decide what is your deepest need. In his infinite wisdom he will give you that which will be a blessing, not an evil, to you. When you go to God in prayer, if you are truly sensitive to his spiritual presence, there will be times when all your problems and desires and longings will be forgotten in the realization that God is with you and nothing else really matters. Then, when your prayer is ended, you will be so undergirded with spiritual power that you will wonder why you were ever baffled by these problems.

Keep alive in your heart an awareness of the divine presence, not only when you are praying but throughout the day, and in the midst of this fevered generation you will move with quietness, serenity, and inner strength. The greatest men and women whom the world has known are those who have walked with God.

When you face life's disappointments and temptations and difficulties, there is no stimulus half so great as the assurance that God is with you and that the spiritual forces of the universe are on your side. But this conviction can be yours only as you have sought and found the will of God. Then you will be able to say with the psalmist: " I called upon the Lord in distress: the Lord answered me, and set me free. The Lord is on my side; I will not fear: what can man do unto me? "

【3】

DOES ANYTHING HAPPEN WHEN YOU PRAY?

" And when they had prayed, the place was shaken where they were assembled together."

ACTS 4:31

〔3〕

DOES ANYTHING HAPPEN WHEN
YOU PRAY?

COUNT LEO TOLSTOY, in his book *My Confession*, declares that " a man often believes for years that his early faith is still intact, while at the same time not a trace of it remains in him."

As an illustration of this, he quotes the testimony of a friend. Thirty years earlier this friend knelt in prayer at his bedside while on a hunting expedition with his brother. He made the sign of the cross several times, bowing his head reverently at intervals. When he had completed his prayers, his brother, who had been watching him, remarked, " Ah, so you still keep that up." Not another word was said on the subject, but it was enough to demolish the habit of prayer which he had maintained throughout his life. " His brother's words," said Tolstoy, " were like the push of a finger against a wall ready to tumble over with its own weight."

Nothing remained of his early faith except an empty form. When once he had admitted this to himself, he couldn't continue with his prayers.

Tens of thousands of modern people find themselves in a plight similar to this. Prayer has become for them a meaningless ritual, altogether divorced from reality. Nothing ever happens when they pray. They never expect anything to happen, and according to their faith, or more truly their lack of faith, it is done unto them. Their expectation is realized. It registers zero. If they cease this mechanical practice, it will make no difference whatsoever to their lives, since it is completely devoid of content and significance.

Now there are some who will say: " Why not give up prayer if there be no reality in it? Anyway, have we any right to expect something to happen when we pray? "

A philosophy of religion professor in a well-known Eastern college recently published a book in which he declares that religious practices are harmful to men and women because they accustom them to an attitude of " slavish dependence on God." It weakens man, he suggests, to ascribe to God strength and justice and power. Instead of crediting him with these noble qualities man, he declares, ought to claim them all for himself and so master his world.

I am sure that, to many young students largely inexperienced in life, this must sound very logical and convincing. One can understand why it unsettles the faith of some. Nevertheless, the professor's reasoning is completely fallacious. What so many of the advocates of " the cult of man " cannot see is that true prayer releases the infinite resources of God in the lives of men and women. The detractors of prayer say that the more man exalts God, the emptier and weaker he himself becomes and the less is he able to gain strength and courage.

Well then, let us put their theory to the test. If what they say be true, the more completely an individual is surrendered to God, the weaker he should be. It should make him increasingly a helpless, dependent personality.

Now let us look at the lives of some of the great believers in prayer of the past and of the present. Martin Luther was such a one. He spent a considerable part of each day in prayer. Did his faith make him a weakling? Did belief in prayer sap his strength and courage? Why, that man singlehanded, under God, changed the course of human history!

Phillips Brooks was another. He believed passionately in prayer and unfailingly exalted God. Did this make him helpless and dependent? On the contrary, this spiritual giant of Boston placed the indelible stamp of his own consecrated personality upon the religious life of America.

I shall mention but one more from scores of names that could be cited — this from the life of our own day — Albert Schweitzer, of Africa. He believes firmly in prayer and conducts daily prayer services in his hospital. One of the profoundest convictions of his life is that he was led of Almighty God to undertake his medical career, which has brought untold blessing to the natives of Africa. Has his faith in prayer enfeebled him, making him dependent and powerless? The reverse is true. Where in all the world will you find a nobler representative of humanity? Joseph Fort Newton called him " the greatest soul now upon the earth."

These men, and countless others, went to God in surrender and humility, *but they returned with power, conquering and to conquer*. In that divine-human encounter they experienced an inflow of spiritual strength that made them invincible.

But someone says: " If God has all this to offer, why doesn't he give these blessings to man whether he asks for them or not? If God is all-wise and all-powerful, why should he withhold the best from his human children? " Let me answer this question by proposing some others. Certainly God loves beauty. One cannot look around him in the world without realizing this. Why, then, does he not make it possible for every man to be an artist and create beauty on canvas without the necessity of long years of discipline and study? Again, God loves music, for he created man with a capacity to enjoy it. Why, then, did he not endow every man with musical ability? And God desires intelligence in his children. Jesus said we should love God with the mind as well as with the heart. Why, then, should it be necessary for us to toil for years in school, high school, and college to achieve an education? Why does not everyone possess an education at birth? Answer these three questions and you will have answered the question that prompted them. God has fashioned his universe in complete consistence. There are no contradictions in it. He has placed man in a world where progress is dependent on man's disciplined efforts, his research, his toil, his strivings upward and onward. Whether it be in the realm of discovery and exploration, in medicine's battle against disease, in man's effort to overcome hunger and poverty, or even in his search for God. Always human co-operation is essential if man is to secure the blessings God has in store for him.

It is not otherwise with prayer. " Ask, and it shall be given you," said Jesus; " seek, and ye shall find; knock, and it shall be opened unto you." Ask — seek — knock. It is obvious that human initiative is always required. It holds an important place in the divine economy. Here, then, is a truth about prayer that we must always remember: *Prayer is the divinely appointed means by which man co-operates with God in order to receive spiritual power.*

A well-known American professor addressed an educational convention in New York not long ago. Speaking of the problem of teaching unco-operative youth, he remarked that it makes one " understand what a dynamo feels like when it is discharging into a nonconductor."

What a vivid simile! Immediately I thought of the immense generators and dynamos at Niagara Falls and the high-tension wires that span northern New York, carrying light and power to homes, stores, and the streets of towns and cities. Yet out on the open countryside there may still be found darkened homes. The wires are there, the power is there, but there is no conductor to carry the electric current into the homes. How like so many of our churches, homes, and lives! God's eternal power waits, but there are too many nonconductors frustrating his divine purposes.

Do you recall those verses in Mark's Gospel telling of Jesus' experience in Nazareth — " He could there do no mighty work . . . and he marveled because of their unbelief "? Had the Master temporarily lost his divine power while he was in Nazareth? No, there were too many spiritual nonconductors in his home town, so that God's purposes were hindered.

The secret of the victorious march of the Early Church across the Roman world is found in its belief in and practice of prayer. The book of The Acts says, "And when they had prayed, the place was shaken where they were assembled together." Something always happened in the Early Church when these people prayed. It should be obvious that it wasn't the building that was shaken — that would mean only a repair job on the structure. The disciples were shaken by the Spirit of God. What produced this powerful effect? The explanation is given two verses beyond: "With great power gave the apostles witness of the resurrection of the Lord Jesus." The Greek word for power is *dynamis*, from which our words "dynamic" and "dynamo" come. These early Christians were spiritual conductors, and God manifested himself mightily in their lives. The need of the hour is more prayer groups in our churches, that they may become centers of pulsating, dynamic, spiritual power.

All that I have said can be verified in your own experience. Ask God to bring you a deep and abiding blessing, to manifest his power in you, and then be alert to watch for the answer to your prayer. What may we expect? Dr. Alexis Carrel, who has written so frequently on prayer, answers this question. Here are some of the results: "Increased physical buoyancy, greater intellectual vigor, moral stamina, better human relations, and complete and harmonious assembly of body, mind, and spirit which gives the frail human reed its unshakable strength." This is not a clergyman speaking but a world-renowned physician.

Dr. Carrel does not stand alone in his advocacy of prayer. After Captain Eddie Rickenbacker returned from his unforgettable experience of twenty-one days adrift in the Pacific, he was called upon to address a large group of disabled veterans in a rehabilitation hospital. What do you suppose was the message he brought these men? Only incidentally he touched upon employment and business opportunities for the disabled. The keynote of his address is found in one sentence: "Men, if you have not had an experience of God in your life, my advice is to get busy and get yourself one."

An experience of God! That is, of course, man's most urgent need. All other needs are secondary to this. We look around us and see multiplying nervous ailments, moral standards sagging and collapsing, and the disappointment of our hopes for world understanding and peace. Multitudes are becoming disheartened and anxious. What we need above all else is an experience of God that will enable us to face life unafraid.

Archbishop Richard Trench's sonnet has still a message for our day:

" Lord, what a change within us one short hour
    Spent in Thy presence will avail to make!
    What heavy burdens from our bosoms take!
    What parched grounds refresh as with a shower!
We kneel, and all around us seems to lower;
    We rise, and all, the distant and the near,
    Stands forth in sunny outline, brave and clear;

We kneel, how weak! we rise, how full of power!
Why, therefore, should we do ourselves this wrong,
Or others — that we are not always strong." [4]

[4] From *The World's Great Religious Poetry*, edited by
Caroline M. Hill, p. 416. The Macmillan Company, 1936.

⟦4⟧

WILL YOUR PRAYERS FOR OTHERS AFFECT THEIR LIVES?

"Moreover as for me, God forbid that I should sin against the Lord in ceasing to pray for you. . . ."

I SAMUEL 12:23

[4]

WILL YOUR PRAYERS FOR OTHERS AFFECT THEIR LIVES?

DECEMBER 12, 1901, is a memorable date in the history of invention. On that day a renowned electrical scientist sat in a small shack not far from the city of St. John's, Newfoundland. Eagerly he bent over an electric instrument that from time to time gave forth a little sputter. Nothing intelligible came from it. Then suddenly, unmistakably, three short, sharp dots sounded repeatedly. It was the letter S in the Morse code — the S that is used in the now famous S O S call. Joy glowed in the face of Signor Marconi, for he was the first man to hear a wireless message from across the Atlantic Ocean. He knew that the problem was now solved, and that soon radio would not only bridge the oceans but would encircle the earth.

To me, that thrilling episode is a parable of prayer. Prayer is a message flung across the space between earth and heaven; or, more accurately, it is a communication with that spiritual world that enfolds and interpenetrates the physical.

There are forces in the universe, invisible forces, that man may tap and by which he can add to his native resources of mind and body. Drawing upon these spiritual forces, man finds his strength increased, his physical powers vitalized, his thinking clarified, and his whole being suffused with divine energy.

It was of this that Dr. Glover was doubtless thinking when he said that the early Christians " out-lived, out-thought and out-died " the pagans of their time. Men of prayer have always been men of power, for prayer is a linking of the human with the divine. When Henry M. Stanley, the noted explorer, emerged from the jungles and fever swamps of Africa, he said that prayer had made him stronger morally and physically than his nonpraying companions. And he added, " It did not blind my eyes, or dull my mind, or close my ears, but on the contrary it gave me confidence."

As a well-known American preacher has put it, " Prayer can be drums and bugles to one's spirit." It infuses courage into fainting hearts. It adds a new dimension to life. It makes available inexhaustible resources.

Lord Morley, in his life of William Ewart Gladstone, says that he discovered in Gladstone's papers a private diary in which he recorded his inner life of prayer. The great statesman drew courage and strength from the environing presence of God. On the occasion of one of his most important speeches in the British House of Commons, while he was waiting to catch the speaker's eye, his lips moved constantly. Members of the House thought that he was rehearsing his speech, but in his private diary he says he was engaged in prayer. He was quoting a passage from The Psalms: " Give thy strength unto thy servant, O Lord. Give thy strength unto thy servant." When at last his magnificent voice sounded throughout the House of Commons, it was not just William Ewart Gladstone speaking — it was Gladstone undergirded of God.

There are few better ways of praying than sending up your prayer upon the wings of one of the great affirmations of the Bible. Here is an instance of it: " The Lord is my light and my salvation; whom shall I fear? the Lord is the strength of my life; of whom shall I be afraid? " Yes! prayer can be " drums and bugles " to your spirit.

Now, all that we have been discussing up to this point is prayer for oneself. This is only one aspect of prayer. Perhaps we can all say, " Lord what a change *within us* one short hour spent in thy presence will avail to make! " [5] Within us — yes — but what about outside us? Can prayer effect changes there?

There are some who vigorously deny this possibility. One of these was the German philosopher Immanuel Kant. He wrote, " It is at once an absurd and presumptuous delusion to try, by insistent importunity of prayer, whether God might not be deflected from the plan of his wisdom to provide some momentary advantage for us."

Kant, and most of those who deny the possibility of petitionary prayer, are oppressed by the idea of nature as a closed system which imprisons personality. But the reverse of this is the truth. A law-abiding universe becomes the servant of the personality. Man's powers have not been decreased but vastly enhanced by universal law.

This truth was borne in upon me one day as I stood in St. Peter's Square in Rome and gazed at the majestic

[5] *Ibid.*

cathedral called after the fisherman apostle. Suddenly the
thought dawned upon me: That vast structure was born
in the mind of a man. It was Michelangelo whose brain
conceived that glorious dome and that stately façade.
Oftentimes in Florence he had gazed at Brunelleschi's
dome on the *duomo* and dreamed of constructing one that
might somewhat remotely resemble it. Then one day he
saw his hopes realized in the vast cathedral of St. Peter's
at Rome.

But this achievement was possible only because Michelangelo knew that the law of physics and dynamics
would not change overnight and could be made the serv-
ants of his will. So human personality is stamped on that
great cathedral.

In a multitude of different ways man projects his will
deep into the realm of physical laws. He defies gravity in
his stratoliners and hydrodynamics in his submarines. He
sends his voice and his pictures, through the ether, around
the earth. The laws of the universe have not imprisoned
him. They have released him, enhancing all his powers. I
cannot but believe that man's limited control of nature's
forces is a counterpart of God's unlimited powers, for the
whole universe is the expression of His will.

This does not mean, as Immanuel Kant suggests, that
prayer is an attempt to deflect God " from the plan of his
wisdom." That, in truth, was the interpretation put on
prayer in the childhood of our race — and it is a viewpoint
still held by people who are spiritually immature. But
those who have been sitting at the feet of Christ know
from his example that prayer is not overcoming God's

reluctance but, rather, co-operating with his willingness.

Intercessory prayer is doubly blessed. It blesses him who prays. Its unfailing answer is that he meets with God. In addition, it enlarges his heart, quickens his compassion, and makes him more Godlike. In the second place, it blesses him for whom he prays. This is true even if not a single specific gift is requested on behalf of that person. Saint Teresa, who was so resourceful in prayer, asked nothing for those for whom she prayed but simply " held them up in the light " of God, that he might cleanse or heal them as he willed. When once we have recognized petitionary prayer for what it is — a God-appointed way for releasing his divine power — we may pray for whomever or whatever we choose, for the issue remains with Him who is infinite wisdom and everlasting love.

Contrast Abraham's prayer for Sodom with Lot's prayer for himself. The great patriarch prayed earnestly for the salvation of others — the undeserving townsfolk of Sodom. Lot offered a selfish petition for his own personal comfort and safety.

Abraham's prayer is a remarkable spiritual achievement, especially when we remember that it was composed more than a thousand years before the birth of Christ. Note several important elements in it:

1. It is the first recorded prayer in the Bible.
2. It is offered in behalf of others.
3. It is a prayer for a whole city.
4. It is uttered on behalf of an indifferent and rebellious people.
5. It is made in the spirit of boldness and yet of humility.
6. Abraham's petition was not granted.

The fact that Abraham's petition was not granted does not invalidate prayer. As Charles E. Jefferson has said, *" We must always remember that God has given to every soul and to every city the responsibility of deciding what its character and destiny shall be."* The city of Sodom was itself the supreme obstacle to the answer of Abraham's prayer. It chose the way that leads to destruction.

What a responsibility rests on us in this ministry of intercession! When we fail to employ it, only God knows the spiritual loss that is suffered by ourselves, by those we love, and by the world as a whole.

James says, " Ye have not, because ye ask not." And Isaiah pictures the divine amazement at human neglect: " And he saw that there was no man, and wondered that there was no intercessor."

Samuel the prophet goes beyond even these: he says that neglect to pray for others is not merely crass indifference to their spiritual welfare but an outright sin. " Moreover as for me," says Samuel, " God forbid that I should sin against the Lord in ceasing to pray for you."

One cannot study the life of Jesus without seeing that he regarded prayer as a mighty spiritual power by which the Church would be enabled to triumph over every foe and finally win the world for him. If we falter today, if the Kingdom tarries, it is because we shamefully neglect intercessory prayer.

Some years ago I was invited to conduct a special preaching mission in a Western city. The appeal was signed by every minister of that city. They urged the necessity of the mission on two grounds: first, the spiritual indifference of church people; and, secondly, the divisions and discords that existed among the churches. I accepted the invitation on two conditions: that the intervening four months would be spent by these churches in prayer, and that all the ministers would sit on the platform each night of our meetings. These stipulations were accepted. I arrived at that Western city on a Saturday night and was greeted on the railroad platform by the chairman of the mission. He said, " I don't want to belittle anything that you may accomplish in this preaching mission, but I want to tell you that if you took the next train back home we should already have been blessed, because the prayers that have been offered during the last four months have already stirred the whole city."

In my entire ministry I have never known anything comparable to the spiritual power that was present in those meetings. People began assembling at six o'clock for services that would open at eight, and in the crowded auditorium with two overflow congregations the hush of God fell night after night and hundreds of lives were committed to him. Never in all my experience did I find it easier to preach. The conditions had been fulfilled for the release of divine power and God opened the windows of heaven and poured out a blessing on a people whose hearts had been made ready by the ministry of intercessory prayer.

What a tragedy that we should ever be impoverished when God's resources are ample for all! Dr. John Henry Jowett prophetically described our present situation: " The multitude is not sick of Jesus; it is only sick of his feeble and bloodless representatives. When once again a great Church appears, a Church with the Lord's name in her forehead, a Church with fine muscular limbs and face seamed with the marks of sacrifice, the multitude will turn their feet to the way of God's commandments." [6]

[6] *The Transfigured Church*, by J. H. Jowett. Fleming H. Revell Company, 1910.

[5]

THE LORD'S PRAYER INTERPRETED

" *After this manner therefore pray ye: Our Father which art in heaven, Hallowed be thy name.*"

MATTHEW 6:9

⟦5⟧

THE LORD'S PRAYER INTERPRETED

ONE DAY, some years since, Pachmann the Russian pianist gave a recital in Albert Hall. He was in his eightieth year. Ten thousand persons, overflowing the vast auditorium, listened in breathless silence to his exquisite interpretation of Chopin.

Afterward in her home, our hostess asked her daughter, who was an accomplished musician, to play something for us. Still under the spell of the master, she replied: " Who could play after Pachmann? "

That's exactly the way the disciples felt about prayer after they had come upon Jesus in the midst of his devotions. It was his custom to rise a great while before day and betake himself to some mountain solitude where he would talk with his Heavenly Father. Whenever his followers missed him in the morning, they knew that he was off to some upland oratory communing with God.

One day they sought him in a nearby mountain retreat. Climbing a narrow, winding pathway at daybreak, they met a shepherd. " Have you seen anyone abroad on the mountain this morning? " they asked. And the guardian of the flock replied: " Aye, while the night was yet on the mountain, one passed in the darkness. He went up yonder."

Pressing on, in the shelter of a huge rock, they found the Master still kneeling in prayer. The dew was on his garments and on his hair, but his face was transfigured with the glory of heaven. In rapt silence the disciples listened to his converse with his Heavenly Father as he spoke words such as never man spoke. When he ceased, one of them — I think it must have been Peter — said, "Lord, teach us to pray."

Of course they were all praying men, but having seen and heard Jesus at prayer, they felt they were less than novices.

In response to their request, Jesus took them aside and taught them the greatest prayer ever given to man. In the Early Church it was called simply " the prayer," and was repeated three times daily. It is brief — in its shortest form consisting of only fifty-eight words — recalling the Lord's warning against the long prayers of the Pharisees. It is simple, so that a child's mind can understand it, and at the same time it is profound — as high as heaven and as unfathomable as the mind of God. It is universal. It knows no limitation of race or rank, caste or color. It is a pattern to be followed: " After this manner therefore pray ye." It is also a form to be used: " When ye pray, say, Our Father." It is a summary. As the law of love is a summary of all laws, so this prayer covers all earthly and spiritual needs and all heavenly aspirations. It contains six petitions. Some have said it contains seven, but the seventh, " Deliver us from evil," is but the positive form of the sixth petition — " Lead us not into temptation."

Now these six petitions are equally divided between the things of God and the needs of man. I particularly ask you to notice the order in which these interests are presented in this model prayer.

First, the things of God: the first half of the prayer concerns God's glory, God's Kingdom, and God's will. In a secondary position are the needs of man: bread, forgiveness, and deliverance from temptation. You will not fail to note that of these six petitions only one is concerned with provisions for our physical needs. The other five deal with the things of God and the needs of the soul of man. This is in accord with Jesus' teaching, " Seek ye first the kingdom of God, and his righteousness; and all these things [food, drink, clothing] shall be added unto you."

There is an additional saying attributed to Jesus by Origen, a Christian scholar of the early centuries: " Ask the great things and the little things shall be added unto you; ask the heavenly things and the earthly things shall be added unto you."

You see now how far from the mark most of us are in our praying. We reverse the divine order. We put our needs, our desires, our wishes, first, and God's glory, God's Kingdom, and God's will, last. If the importance of giving priority to the things of God be impressed upon your minds and hearts in this study, it will not have been made in vain.

Now let us look at the six petitions.

First: *Our Father which art in heaven, Hallowed be thy name.* At the very opening of the prayer, we bring in all our fellow men — *our* Father. We shall not ask for ourselves any boon that we would deny to any one of God's children.

How it comforts us to know that *our Father* is Lord of the universe! Dr. J. D. Jones, of Bournemouth, tells of a young lad who remained quite unperturbed on a transatlantic liner in the midst of a fierce storm. A passenger, noting that the boy watched with interest the great rollers approaching the tossing ship, said, " Son, aren't you afraid? " The boy smiled and said: " No, sir. You see, my father is captain."

Our Father which art in heaven! Amid all the storms and upheavals of our earthly life we are unafraid when we remember the sovereign power of our Father.

Hallowed be thy name! Let thy name be reverenced. Walk the streets of New York or any other great city and enter its stores and offices and factories and you will blush to hear how often God's holy name is blasphemed by both men and women.

When Gipsy Smith, the noted evangelist, was on his last visit to New York, he told me of a happening as he passed through one of our great department stores. He heard a lovely-looking salesgirl blaspheme the name of God. In his frank, kindly way the Gipsy turned to her and said, " My dear, those pretty lips of yours were not made to take that holy name in vain."

Thy Kingdom come, is the second petition. End the rule of man and let the rule of God begin. The rule of man, with his selfishness and greed, his hates and fears, has brought only sorrow and suffering, turmoil and tears, to our stricken earth.

> " Our life is like a narrow raft
>   Afloat upon a hungry sea;
> Whereon is but a little space,
> And each man eager for a place
>   Doth thrust his brother in the sea;
> And so the sea is salt with tears,
> And so our life is worn with fears."

O God, let thy Kingdom come and thy rule begin!

The third petition is, *Thy will be done in earth, as it is in heaven.* What a corrective to our selfish ways of praying is this third petition in the Lord's Prayer! Before we have ever begun to mention our human needs, we are bidden to pray — not that we succeed in persuading God to change his divine purposes, but rather that our lives may be brought into harmony with his holy will.

I am reminded of the time when Sir Wilfred Grenfell, on a journey of mercy in the Labrador, was swept out to sea while crossing the ice of a Labrador bay. On the ice pan with him were his dogs. The swift current carried them out into the vast and wandering Atlantic. Having survived a bitter night and seeing, dimly, through snow-blinded eyes, the cliffs of the Labrador steadily receding, Grenfell became calmly reconciled to death. At this grim moment, he said, not a trace of fear was in his heart but the stanza of a hymn repeated itself constantly in his mind:

> " My God, my Father, while I stray
> Far from my home, on life's rough way,

O teach me from my heart to say,
' Thy will be done! ' "

So Jesus instructs us to pray, *Thy will be done in earth, as it is in heaven*. Only when we have prayed for God's glory, God's Kingdom, and God's will are we to turn to our human needs.

And that brings us to the fourth petition: *Give US this day OUR daily bread*. Not for selfish interests do we petition. With our own needs in this petition we remember all God's children everywhere.

How glibly and thoughtlessly we utter these words! I frankly confess to you that I never understood their meaning myself until one day in midwinter, during the economic depression of 1929, I attended a service in a city mission. About a hundred children were there. My attention was attracted to a little lad six or seven years old. When the leader said: " Now, children, let us repeat the Lord's Prayer," this little boy had to roll up the sleeves of his coat in order to clasp his hands together as their leader instructed them to do. You see, it was a pass-me-down coat that his brother, three or four years older, had worn. His shoes also were far too big for him, and his toes protruded through the broken leather. I watched him as he recited the Lord's Prayer, noting his wan face and his little undernourished body. When he came to these words, *Give us this day our daily bread*, there was a lump in my throat and in one flash of illumination I knew why Jesus gave us that prayer. When we think of the empty rice bowls in Korea and India and, yes, in Communist China, we all know what he meant.

A professor of philosophy in one of our Eastern colleges says that man will no longer need this prayer when he is able to produce enough to feed all the inhabitants of the globe. What a naïve assumption! The selfish hearts of men will need this prayer until God's Kingdom has come and his will is done on earth as it is in heaven.

In the fifth petition we say, " *Forgive us our debts, as we forgive our debtors.*" Matthew uses the word " debts." Luke's version says, " Forgive us our sins." A considerable percentage of Christendom uses the words, " Forgive us our trespasses," though the word " trespasses " does not occur in either of the two versions of the Lord's Prayer given by the Evangelists. But whatever word we use, the meaning of the petition is abundantly clear. Indeed, it is all too clear for our small hearts.

When Jesus finished teaching his disciples this prayer, according to Matthew he added an explanatory word. He said, " If ye forgive not men their trespasses, neither will your Father forgive your trespasses." Why this repetition? Because he saw the jealousy and anger and unforgiveness in the hearts of his own disciples as they disputed as to which of them was greatest.

In the presence of John Wesley on one occasion, a man said of another, " I shall never forgive the man who did this injury to me." Wesley turned and remarked to him, " Then, my brother, I hope that you will never sin, since if you sin you will stand in need of the divine forgiveness."

When you come before God in prayer, pause long enough to look closely and honestly at the root causes of the grudge you bear against another or the resentments that you cherish, whether they be real or imagined. Then ask God to show you how much of that hurt you received is due to your own attitude and your own lack of the spirit of Christ. When you have so examined yourself, the inspired words of Holy Scripture will sound in your soul like heavenly music: "Let all bitterness, and wrath, and anger, and clamor, and evil speaking, be put away from you, with all malice: And be ye kind one to another, tender-hearted, forgiving one another, even as God for Christ's sake hath forgiven you."

Then, and then only, will you be able honestly and sincerely to pray, "*Forgive us our debts, as we forgive our debtors.*"

And now we reach the final petition: *Lead us not into temptation, but deliver us from evil.* I suppose that this petition has provoked more perplexity and bewilderment among Christian people than any other of the six that make up the Lord's Prayer. Why should we ask God not to lead us into temptation? Is there any possibility that he would tempt us to do evil? Let us be clear on this one thing: God does not stand on the side of evil, enticing men to sin, for, as James truly says, "God cannot be tempted with evil, neither tempteth he any man." Part of our difficulty is because the word "tempt" did not originally mean "seduce," "solicit," "entice"; rather, it meant "to try," "to make test of." This is the form in which the word may be found repeatedly in both the Old and the New Testament. Abraham was tried in the offering up of Isaac. Job was tested by his misfortunes. In both cases the Hebrew word sometimes translated "tempted" is used. Again, when Jesus asked Philip where they could buy bread for the multitude in the desert, the Evangelist writes, " And this he said to prove Philip: for he himself knew what he would do." The word " prove " is the same Greek word as " tempt." But chiefly we read that after his baptism our Lord was led by the Spirit into the wilderness to be " tempted," that is, to be tried or tested.

This is one of the most important petitions in the Lord's Prayer. It is a plea in which man expresses his humility — his mistrust of himself. He declares his awareness of his own weaknesses. Moral testing may be a necessary part of his spiritual development, but he humbly asks God to be near him in the hour of trial and to preserve him from evil. So these words bring this glorious prayer to a close: *Lead us not into temptation, but deliver us from evil.*

The Early Church in its liturgy, added a doxology, which was widely used even in the first century of the Christian Era: *For thine is the kingdom, and the power, and the glory.* This is taken from David's doxology in I Chron. 29:11: " Thine, O Lord, is the . . . power, and the glory and . . . the kingdom."

Dr. William Osler years ago told the students of Yale, " Begin the day with Christ and his prayer; you will need no other." Osler was right. The whole compass of man's need is included in this matchless prayer. It should always be said slowly, thoughtfully, and reverently, so that the meaning of each petition may sink into our hearts. So shall we grow in spiritual maturity and in the knowledge of our Lord and Master, Jesus Christ.

Our Father which art in heaven, Hallowed be Thy name.
Thy kingdom come. Thy will be done on earth as it is in
    heaven.
Give us this day our daily bread.
And forgive us our debts, as we forgive our debtors.
And lead us not into temptation, but deliver us from evil:
For Thine is the kingdom, and the power, and the glory, for
    ever. AMEN.

【6】

JESUS' PRAYER IN GETHSEMANE

" *And he went a little further, and fell on his face, and prayed, saying, O my Father, if it me possible, let this cup pass from me: nevertheless, not as I will, but as thou wilt.*"

MATTHEW 26:39

JESUS' PRAYER IN GETHSEMANE

MAHATMA GANDHI's dearest friend, Charles F. Andrews, was asked on one occasion, " Can you tell me what is the secret of the powerful influence which Gandhi exerts on India's 350,000,000 people and, indeed, upon the world? " Andrews, a devout Christian, replied: " Obviously it is not his physical presence, for he weighs only about one hundred pounds. It is his spiritual force. He maintains this by constant reliance on prayer. One hour, twice a day, he devotes to prayer, and one day in seven he reserves for complete silence and waiting upon God. This is the secret of his influence."

But all this is far more true of another personality, who towers above men of all generations in His solitary majesty. No one ever walked our earth who prayed more than Jesus.

The question may be raised, If Jesus be the Son of God, why should he need to pray? The answer is, Because he was true man as well as true God. While he had no sinful past to cast its shadow over the present, yet in his human nature he needed the restoring power of prayer and sought it constantly.

73

Prayer meant more to Jesus than food. After long abstinence, when the disciples offered him supplies which they had brought from a nearby village, Jesus answered, " I have meat to eat that ye know not of." Prayer replenished even his physical needs. Again, prayer meant more to Jesus than sleep. When he was utterly wearied by unremitting toil, he found in prayer a greater refreshment even than slumber. We read that he rose up " a great while before day, . . . and departed into a solitary place, and there prayed."

It would seem, as Dr. James Stalker suggests, that when Jesus arrived in a Palestinian town, his first thought was of the shortest road to a mountain, that in its natural solitudes he might be undisturbed in prayer. " He went out, and departed into a solitary place, and there prayed."

We find that Jesus prayed with special concentration before taking each important step in his life. When the time came to select from among his followers the twelve men who would become his disciples and apostles, he spent the entire previous night in a mountain alone with God. He gave himself to prayer at the commencement of his ministry in the hour of baptism. He was in the midst of prayer with three of his disciples on a mountaintop when he was transfigured with the reflected glory of heaven, and just before he informed his disciples that he was going to Jerusalem to suffer and die, he turned aside for prayer. In the Garden of Gethsemane, beneath the olive trees, occurred what was perhaps the bitterest conflict in his whole life, and through prayer he gained the victory. Finally, on Calvary with its blasphemies and tortures, he breathed out his life in prayer to his Heavenly Father. The practice that prevailed throughout his life was strong in the hour of death and brought to him an unbroken peace that not all the enmity of evil men could take away.

The many instances of prayer in the life of our Lord, significant though they be, pale before the glory, the mystery, and the touching intimacy of his threefold petition in the Garden of Gethsemane. The Last Supper was ended, Judas had gone off on his mission of betrayal, and the long-smoldering hate of the Pharisees and Sadducees was about to burst into flame. From many an upper room where families and kindred were meeting together the light of lamps shone forth. In the streets the sound of many feet on the pavement betokened unusual excitement. This would be an eventful Passover Feast.

The eleven disciples, with Jesus at their head, descended from the city gates into the Valley of Jehoshaphat and crossed the brook Kidron to the Mount of Olives. Bishop Lightfoot tells us that all the blood drained from the Temple altars flowed into the Kidron. There is good reason to believe that at the time of the Passover, and perhaps even as Jesus and his disciples crossed the Kidron in the moonlight, the stream was running red. One wonders if John the Baptist's prophecy came into the mind of our Lord in that dread hour: "Behold the Lamb of God which taketh away the sin of the world!"

The place to which he led His disciples was familiar to all of them. It was an olive orchard containing an oil press. The name "Gethsemane" means, simply, "oil press." To this secluded retreat Jesus and his disciples had come each night to escape the turmoil and dissensions of Jerusalem. Now, with the dread weight of impending events pressing on his soul, our Lord sought the shelter of this well-loved place where the olive leaves would afford him concealment, despite the paschal moon shining brightly in the midnight sky. Eight of the disciples he stationed just within the Garden gate, saying, " Sit ye here, while I . . . pray." Then, taking with him Peter and James and John, with whom he had shared so many intimate experiences, he went into the deeper recesses of the orchard. Mark says that he " began to be sore amazed, and to be very heavy," which in modern language means, " He became greatly bewildered and troubled." It frightened the disciples to see their Master so distressed. Only an hour earlier in the upper room he had appeared calm and triumphant, but now he is swept by a storm of tumultuous emotions. He said: " My soul is exceeding sorrowful unto death: tarry ye here, and watch." Then he withdrew from them a little distance and fell on the ground and prayed. He wished to be alone. With only God as his companion he wanted to fight to a finish the conflict raging within his own soul.

Recently, in the memoirs of Prime Minister Churchill, I read his description of one of the greatest naval defeats of World War II, second only to the disaster of Pearl Harbor. While the warships that had survived the Japanese attack were hastening to United States ports on the Pacific coast, Prime Minister Churchill rejoiced that Britain had two of her newest and finest warships at Singapore — the

Prince of Wales and the *Repulse*. He planned to offer them to the American Government so that they might join the remainder of the Pacific fleet, believing that this gesture would knit together the English-speaking world. Just at this particular time a telephone message came from the first sea lord. In a choking voice he said: " Sir, I regret to report that the *Prince of Wales* and the *Repulse* have both been sunk and the commanding officer, Admiral Sir Tom Phillips, is drowned with more than a thousand of his men." Churchill writes: " So I put the telephone down. I was thankful to be alone. In all the war I never received a more direct shock."

It is quite evident that the man of iron had broken down and wept. " I was thankful to be alone."

We all desire to be alone when the storm comes down upon our souls and we are battling our way through. We need time to think, time to pull ourselves together, time to rally our scattered resources. If Churchill wanted no man to see his agony, there were a thousand more reasons why Jesus desired solitude as he wrestled in his soul with the stark, grim, brutal fact of the crucifixion. From his lips there came the cry: " Abba, Father, all things are possible unto thee; take away this cup from me: nevertheless, not what I will, but what thou wilt."

As we read of these happenings, we fear, even in imagination, to look upon the scene or to listen to the Master's words. As he prayed in agony, we are told by the Evangelists that his sweat was as great drops of blood falling to the ground. " Abba, Father, all things are possible unto thee; take away this cup from me." We cannot comprehend this scene. It is beyond our understanding. We can but listen to this agonized petition from the lips of the prostrate Jesus in wonderment and silence.

On one occasion, as Dr. John Henry Jowett was speaking of Jesus' prayer in Gethsemane, he said: " And now I lead you by a path that I almost fear to tread." With a like humility we walk today. At least we can say with confidence that it was not merely the fear of death that weighed on the soul of Jesus. Many days before he had faced and conquered that. What could this awful burden have been that crushed the holy, sinless Jesus to the earth? Was it the weight of all the world's sin and anguish that pressed on his divine consciousness? Was the cup that he dreaded the guilt and shame of our stricken race?

> " Desperate tides of the whole world's anguish
> Forced through the channels of a single heart. " [7]

No wonder the Master wanted to be alone in this terrible hour of testing — alone with God.

And yet, at the same time, Jesus wanted not to be alone. He brought the three disciples with him into the depth of the Garden that they might watch with him, that they might pray with him, that he might have the comfort of human comradeship. " Watch ye here," he said, " while I go and pray yonder."

What an inexpressible comfort in a time of tragedy, temptation, or overwhelming grief to know that the pulse of some human heart is beating in sympathy with our own! That lesson was taught me unforgettably some years

[7] Frederic W. H. Myers.

ago. When I was in my middle teens my mother " fell on sleep." Suddenly it seemed as though the bottom of the whole world had fallen out, and a sixteen-year-old lad was lost in grief and loneliness. When the congregation had gathered for the funeral service, I looked up in amazement to see a friend enter, an American businessman who had come to Canada some months before to do volunteer work for the Y.M.C.A. It was he who had led me to Christ. He came and sat beside me. Somehow, in the good providence of God, he had returned to this little Canadian town just in the hour of my greatest need. He said not a word, but gripped my hand in a warm clasp. At the close of the service we shook hands in farewell. I have never seen him since that day, but to the end of my life I shall remember what he did for me.

Amid the darkness and loneliness of Gethsemane, three times Jesus stretched forth his hand to the disciples, but there was no answering clasp. They were asleep — asleep with weariness and grief. They failed their Master when he needed them most, when he yearned for the grip of a comradely hand. In the darkness of Gethsemane he went to the sleeping men and aroused them saying, " Could ye not watch with me one hour? " They had let him go love's redeeming way alone.

The uncertainty that for a while was manifested in his prayer is now gone. A note of assurance sounds in his voice as he prays, " Nevertheless, my Father, not my will but thine be done." A great peace falls upon his spirit as Jesus yields himself in complete submission to the Father's will.

Now the silence of the Garden is broken by the voices of approaching men. The glare of torches penetrates deep into the shadows and is reflected from swords and spears. " Rise," said Jesus to his disciples, " let us be going: Behold, he that betrayeth me is at hand."

The Roman soldiers and the Temple police who had come to take him are suddenly filled with confusion. They see twelve men instead of the One they sought. Judas steps forward to give them the prearranged signal and Jesus interrupts him, asking, " Judas, betrayest thou the Son of man with a kiss? "

Turning to the captain of the guard, he inquires, " Whom seek ye? " and the soldier replies, " Jesus the Nazarene." Stepping forth from the shadows of the Garden into the full light of the torches, Jesus declares, " I am He." His sudden appearance, so tall and majestic, as he approaches them fills the soldiers and the mob with an unreasoning terror and recoiling, in panic, they fall back on the ground.

After his prayer in the Garden of Gethsemane the heart of Jesus was at peace. He was brought before Annas the high priest, and Herod the king, and Pilate the Roman governor. Those who were present on these occasions, seeing his kingly majesty, felt that the Prisoner was really the judge and that his judges were the prisoners at the bar. He was the one calm person at each of these unjust and hate-filled trials. In majestic silence he met the worst that cruel men could do to him in the knowledge that he was fulfilling the Heavenly Father's will. On the cross, amid its blasphemies and tortures, its nakedness and death, he was heard to say: " Father, forgive them; for they know not what they do."

How hopeless seemed our Lord's cause in that dark hour on Calvary. But now Pilate is forgotten. Caiaphas and Annas are remembered no more. The Roman Empire, so all-powerful in that day, has disappeared but Jesus Christ is still supreme! He demonstrated to the world the redemptive power of vicarious suffering. When he was reviled he reviled not again. When he suffered he threatened not. " He took upon himself a burden he did not need to carry. He kept on loving men even while they hated him. He died for men who were unworthy of his sacrifice." The chastisement of the world's peace was upon him and by his stripes we are healed.

{7}

ANSWERING YOUR QUESTIONS
ON PRAYER

" . . . Be ready always to give an answer to every man that asketh you a reason of the hope that is in you. . . . "

I Peter 3:15

{7}

ANSWERING YOUR QUESTIONS
ON PRAYER

DR. RUFUS JONES, the beloved Quaker philosopher, received a letter from a man who objected to the emphasis he laid on intelligence in religion. The critic wrote, " Whenever I go to church I feel like unscrewing my head and placing it under the seat because in a religious meeting I never have use for anything above my collar button."

That man's concept of religion is poles removed from Christianity. Jesus frequently stressed the necessity of using our God-given intelligence in religion as well as in secular matters. On one occasion a lawyer came to him asking, " Which is the great commandment in the law? " Jesus quoted the Deuteronomic law: " Thou shalt love the Lord thy God with all thy heart, and . . . soul, and . . . strength." Now this was quite familiar to his questioner, but Jesus didn't stop there. He added a new dimension to the commandment: " And with all thy mind."

So Peter was not breaking new ground when he wrote to the Christians of his day, " Be ready always to give an answer to every man that asketh you a reason of the hope that is in you."

Intellectual honesty is a prerequisite of true Christianity, and reasonableness one of its chief characteristics. At the same time Christianity recognizes that there are vast areas of human interest and experience that lie beyond reason. The sense of beauty is one of these. The idea of the holy, or the religious sense, is another. While the realization of spiritual reality is beyond reason, it is still reasonable and is manifested chiefly in prayer.

Here are some questions on prayer submitted by listeners to this series of addresses.

First: "*Should we pray for fine weather on Sundays so that more people will attend church?*" The trouble with this proposal is that it attacks the problem at too low a level. The questioner is unaware of the human problem involved. I confess that there was a time in my early ministry when I prayed for good weather on Sundays. After one had put many hours of thought and study into a sermon, it was understandably discouraging if one had to address it to empty pews. However, I stopped praying about the weather when I discovered that if it were especially good people stayed away from church saying, "It's too fine today to be indoors." There is a much more fundamental way to meet the problem of church attendance. It is to pray that our people will develop a loyalty to God, his Church, and his Kingdom, that will not fluctuate with every change of weather. Unless we achieve this happy result, a barometer or a weather vane, rather than a cross, would be a fitting symbol for Christians.

The question which I have attempted to answer may appear to some to be trifling, but it contains implications that have a bearing upon every walk of life. One lesson the answer should teach us is never to expect God to alter the laws of the universe in order to accomplish a purpose that can be achieved by correcting our own casual and undisciplined habits of living.

The second question was asked in different forms by several persons: " *What are we to make of passages in the New Testament that seem to imply that if we have sufficient faith, anything we ask of God will be given us?* " Among the passages cited are these:

" What things soever ye desire, when ye pray, believe that ye receive them, and ye shall have them."

" If ye abide in me, and my words abide in you, ye shall ask what ye will, and it shall be done unto you."

" Whatsoever ye shall ask in my name, that will I do."

Does it not seem as if our Lord were issuing blank checks signed with his name, guaranteeing whatever we desire? If this were literally true, it would endanger the orderliness of the universe and plunge us into chaos. Tens of thousands of contradictory prayers are offered every minute of every day and night. In order to grant them all, God would have to resign his government of the universe. As a matter of fact, however, we have no right to draw such conclusions from these promises of our Lord. Always there is a condition — a qualification — either explicitly stated or implied.

Let me single out these conditions. " Believe that ye receive them, and ye shall have them." After all, this makes a tremendous demand upon us. It means that our faith in God must be complete and unreserved. We must surrender ourselves wholly to God's will in trust and obedience. Anyone who achieves this submission need not fear that he will make a wrong request. But how many of us, I wonder, have attained that high point of spiritual development?

Examining the second verse we find that people often lay all the stress on the *promise:* " Ye shall ask what ye will, and it shall be done unto you." But that pledge is made by our Lord only if the preceding *condition* is fulfilled: " If ye abide in me, and my words abide in you." If we abide in Christ and his words abide in us, we shall desire nothing contrary to the divine will.

Now look at the third verse: " Whatsoever ye shall ask in my name." The word " name " in the Bible means " spirit " or " power." This condition affirms that we must make our requests in the " spirit " of Christ. Now, if we ask anything in the spirit of Christ, we signify our acceptance of God's will. Then the promise is fulfilled: " That will I do." Never forget, therefore, that a condition, is either explicitly stated or implied by Jesus in what, at first glance, may appear to be sweeping and ill-considered promises.

" In that case," someone says, " doesn't it mean that our intercessory prayers are all tentative and provisional? " No! Some of them necessarily are tentative, and for very good reasons. God will not grant us a personal request that would defeat his plan for others of his human family. When this has been said, however, let it be remembered that there are great areas of human life and experience in which we do not have to be tentative or provisional be-

cause there God's will has already been made known.
Wherever God has made specific promises to his children,
we need not say, " If it be thy will."

What are the experiences of life covered by the promises of God? Here are some of them: that his divine forgiveness is available to all penitent men and women; that
spiritual power is given to those who seek to overcome
temptation; that courage, born of trust in God, garrisons
all who seek to master life's difficulties and disappointments; that inner strength, serenity, and peace will flow
into the hearts of those who seek them with expectant
faith. All these inestimable blessings God has promised
to us. According to Jesus, if we truly believe that we have
received these gifts, they will be ours.

A third questioner asks: " *What is one to do if he feels
that his prayers do not reach even the ceiling of his room
— that they are hollow, meaningless words? In that event,
should one continue to pray?* " Let it not be forgotten that
all of us, without exception, are subject to moods of the
soul. During a depressed mood, we may feel spiritually impoverished. Such moods are clouds in our spiritual sky.
But clouds in the sky do not mean that the sun no longer
exists. All the saints and mystics of history at some time or
another have suffered from periodic discouragement. Even
such spiritual giants of the Bible as Moses, Elijah, Jere-
miah, Paul, met depressed moments during which it
seemed as if evil were finally victorious. But these heroes
of faith refused to surrender to their moods. They would
not permit a temporary depression to become chronic.
Paul said in a letter to Timothy, " Be instant in season,

out of season." In other words, " Keep up your devotions
whether you feel like doing it or not." Dean Goulburn
echoed the apostle's advice when he wrote, " When you
cannot pray as you would, pray as you can." That is sound
advice. The thought of God's presence and God's power
is one of the most potent remedies for depressed spirits.
Never give up prayer!

The fourth questioner asks: " *Will you explain in
greater detail what you mean by the assertion, ' No true
prayer ever goes unanswered ' ? "* Let me put the statement
in another way. When God cannot answer affirmatively a
man's petition, he answers the man. The very fact that
one meets with God is itself an answer to prayer. But more
than this, when it is not the divine will that our circumstances be changed, God often makes a change *in ourselves,* and that is an answer to prayer. Paul's thorn in
the flesh illustrates this. Thrice he prayed that he might
be delivered from this physical malady, but the thorn in
the flesh remained. Nevertheless, the man was answered
and Paul was given such an accession of divine strength
and courage that the malady no longer mattered. Which
would have been the greater example to Christians across
nineteen centuries? Paul freed of his malady, or Paul
burdened with a physical weakness and crying: " When I
am weak, then am I strong. . . . I glory in my infirmity
that the power of God may rest on me "? God did not
grant the apostle's petition, but he answered the man.

Take again a more recent example. Adoniram Judson,
Massachusetts-born missionary of the last century, prayed
to be sent to India, but he was compelled by circumstances

to go to Burma. He prayed for his wife's life, but buried her and their two children. He prayed for release from a Burma prison, but was kept there eleven terrible months, chained and miserable.

The missionary's petitions were not answered, but God answered the man. Judson rendered immeasurable service to the Kingdom of God in Burma, and his Burmese-English dictionary is a monument of fine scholarship. This is what Judson wrote on the subject of prayer: " I never prayed sincerely and earnestly for anything but it came . . . no matter at how distant a day. Somehow, in some shape — probably the last I should have devised — it came." How wonderfully the man was answered!

The fifth question asks: " *By what means can prayer offered for others affect their lives?* " The answer, it seems to me, lies in the realm of psychological laws. Dean Bosworth points out that most of the prayers we ask of God on behalf of others can be answered, if God possesses power to put a thought into a human mind. When I preached this sermon, I put thoughts into my listeners' minds by using words as a vehicle. But there are other ways of reaching minds. Science today is exploring the whole realm of extrasensory perception. Most educated people believe that we can influence each other's thinking to some degree at least without any sensory contact. There appears to be evidence that God influences the minds of men, and in so doing alters the course of events. In this matter we are embarrassed, not by the scarcity of supporting material, but by its abundance.

Some years ago I heard Dr. John R. Mott tell of an unusual experience that befell him in India. He addressed student bodies at the various university centers. The halls were crowded with Mohammedans, Buddhists, Parsees, Jains, who, without exception, were antagonistic. At times he found himself physically and mentally wearied by this opposition. Finally he arrived at Madras. The students of the university met in a great pavilion. As he addressed them, everything appeared to be going against him. The hostility of his audience was unrestrained. Every time Dr. Mott mentioned the name of Jesus the students responded with hisses. He became so discouraged that he was ready to quit. At this moment he noticed students getting up throughout the audience and leaving the auditorium. He assumed that it was because of their antagonism to his message. Then something happened. A hush came over the student body, and with it an increasing attention to his words. Finally, in response to his closing appeal, scores of non-Christian students came forward, signifying the surrender of their lives to Jesus Christ. Later Dr. Mott learned that the students he had seen leaving various parts of the hall were Indian Christians. They had gone out to join an impromptu prayer meeting and unitedly besought God to intervene — to let his Spirit come mightily upon the meeting. The prayer was answered in a hush of divine power. Dr. Mott said, " Even as Christ stilled the tempest nineteen hundred years ago on the Sea of Galilee, so in modern India he quieted the storm of antagonism and hate in that Madras pavilion."

Yes, prayers offered on behalf of others can affect their lives. As the result of this series of addresses I trust that multitudes who have listened to them on the radio or have read them in print will give themselves to prayer — prayer for our President and the members of Congress; prayer for all the people of our far-flung country; prayer for our churches and ministers and office bearers, that they may be filled with divine zeal and power to make our churches more effective in the life of the nation; prayer for our homes and our loved ones; prayer for ourselves, that we may be filled with inner serenity and spiritual power with which to meet whatever life has in store for us. Prayers such as these, offered in expectant faith, will not be made in vain. As a result, out of the stress and turmoil of the present will emerge a more Christian America and a finer world.